THIS IS AMERICA

INTRODUCTION

In 1607 the British founded their first colony who was Virginia. Then from 1607 to 1732 the British established 13 colonies were located on the Atlantic coast of North America. Following Virginia (1607), New York (1626), Massachusetts (1630), Maryland (1633), Rhode Island (1636), Connecticut (1636), New Hampshire (1638),

Delaware (1638), North Carolina (1653), South Carolina (1663), New Jersey (1664), Pennsylvania (1682), and Georgia (1732).

On April 19, 1775 British soldiers, called lobster backs because of their red coats and minutemen the Colonists militia exchanged gunfire at Lexington and Concord in Massachusetts. Historians described as "the shot heard round the world," it was the beginning of the American Revolution and led to the foundation of a new nation. The American Revolutionary war last 8 years from April 19, 1775 to September 3, 1783. The Treaty of Paris was signed in Paris France by the representatives of King George III of Great Britain and Benjamin Franklin who was the leader of the representatives of the United States of America and Canada. This Treaty of Paris ended officially the American Revolutionary War.

On July 4, 1776, Thomas Jefferson wrote the Declaration of Independence, and the reason why he was chosen, it is because he was eloquent and his ability to write faster than the other five.

On September 17, 1787, our Founding Fathers decided to sign and ratified the United States Constitution. And the one who was chosen by General George Washington to lead the group of three masterminds were Alexander Hamilton, whom wrote 50% of the US Constitution, James

Madison and John Jay both wrote 25% each. And it was Benjamin Franklin who made the motion to sign the document. Three of them refused to sign the document and one of the was George Mason. Then on October 27, 1787 the US Constitution was established and content 27 Amendments and 85 Federalist Papers.

In 1787 the Founding Fathers gathered to wrote the Constitution a set of principles that told how the new nation would be governed. The Founding Fathers wanted a strong and fair national government. And they did not want to form a government that did not allow one person to have too much power or control. With this kind of mindset, they wrote the Constitution to provide for a separation of three branches of the government. The Englishman John Locke first came with the idea, and he only suggested a separation between the Executive and Legislative. The second was the Frenchman Charles-Louis de Secondat, Baron de Montesquieu, added the Judicial branch. Each branch is genuinely equal to each of the others.

* Legislative: Makes laws (Congress, comprised of the House of Representatives and Senate).

* Executive: Carried out laws (President, Vice President, Cabinet and Federal agencies)

* Judicial: Evaluates or interprets laws (Supreme Court and other courts)

On March 4, 1789, the Congress of the United States was established by the new Constitution. This is was the same year when the first President was elected unanimously, and his name was George Washington who led the Continental Army during the Revolutionary War of 1775-1783 against the British. And he led the country between 1789 to 1797 and John Adams was his Vice-President. President George Washington did not have no party designation.

Chapter 1: Words

Our words are powerful, we must use them wisely

only to heal, for prosperity and to bless. Because

with your words you can build or destroy your own

life or the lives of the people who believe in you.

On November 6, 1860, Abraham Lincoln was

elected the sixteenth President of the United States.

His election to the presidency brought fear to the

South and led directly to the breakup of the Union.

Few months after his election 13 states left the

Union. Because they did not want to lose their

privileges to own African American slaves (human

beings) they established 13 Confederate States.

They also elected their President Jefferson Davis.

On April 12, 1861, the North and South were

engrossed in a bloody Civil War.

 Because of the words of Jefferson Davis and his

Vice-President Alexander Hamilton Stephens.

They brain washed even intellectual people, who

attended WestPoint New York (Military Academy)

to follow them. Was fought July 1 to July 3, 1863,

in and around the battlefield of Gettysburg,

Pennsylvania, by Union Army who was led by

General George Gordon Meade and the

Confederate Army who was led by General Robert

E. Lee. The battle involved the largest number of

casualties of the entire war and is often described by historians as the war's turning point. Union casualties in the battle numbered 23 000, while the Confederates had lost some 28 000 men and the Union won the battle.

On November 19, 1863 President Lincoln delivered the 272-word known as the Gettysburg Address at the National Cemetery, in Pennsylvania and states "Fourscore and seven years ago our fathers brought forth, on this continent, a new nation, conceived in liberty, and dedicated to the proposition that all men are created equal. "President Lincoln's used his words in his Gettysburg Address was that the living can honor the wartime dead not with a speech, and rather by continuing to fight for the ideas they gave their lives for.

Between April 12, 1861 to April 9, 1865 over 683,000 Americans died in the conflict. The Civil War maintains the highest American casualty total of any conflict. And the Civil War becomes the costliest war that America has ever fought. All those casualties happen because of the words of few mentally uncappable leaders.

On April 14, 1865 just five days after the ended of the Civil War, around 10:00 p.m. A White actor and a sympathizer of the ex-Confederate Army well known in the White community, named John Wilkes Booth entered the Presidential box at Ford's

Theatre in Washington, D.C, and fatally shot President Abraham Lincoln and he died the next morning at 7:22 a.m. on April 15, 1865. Booth was victim of his own beliefs and the beliefs and words of his leaders, who find someone to manipulated.

On July 2, 1881, James A. Garfield the 20th President of the United States, was fatally shot at the Baltimore and Potomac Railroad Station in Washington, D.C at 9:30 a.m. He died in Elberon, New Jersey, 79 days later September 19, 1881. His assassin was Charles J. Guiteau, the reason why he assassinated the President was revenge against President Garfield for an imagined political debt. And he wanted the Vice-President to invoke the

25th Amendment. This example shows us again how people for false allegations and words they are willing to commit the irreparable.

On September 6, 1901, six months into his second term William McKinley, the 25th President of the United States, was assassinated on the grounds of the Pan-American Exposition at the Temple of Music in Buffalo, New York. He died 8 days later on September 14, 1901. The name of the man who assassinated him was Leon Czolgosz. During the economic Panic of 1893 and turned to anarchism, a political philosophy adhered to by recent assassination of foreign leaders. He regarded President McKinley as a symbol of oppression and was convinced that it was his duty as an anarchist to assassinated.

Once again, this tragic story proved us. Indeed, when vulnerable people tune their thoughts into negative beliefs and listen the wrong leaders their lives shift. After the Assassination of President McKinley, the Congress passed legislation to officially charge the Secret Service with the responsibility for protecting the President.

On November 22, 1963 at 12:30 p.m. John Fitzgerald Kennedy, the 35th President of the United States, was assassinated in Dallas Texas by Lee Harvey Oswald. He was a former U.S. Marine. Who had embraced Marxism and defected for a time to the Soviet Union now known as Russia.

Oswald never stood trial for murder because, when

being taken into custody, he was killed by Jack

Rudy, a distraught Dallas nightclub owner. Like

other similar sad events, Oswald probably was

brainwashed by a bad leader. Whom spray hate

instead of love. And his action cost the life of one

of the youngest and brilliant President.

Chapter 2:

Patriotism

A patriot is someone who loves, defends and supports his or her country. That also can be a person who vigorously supports his country and who is prepared or willing to defend it against enemies or detractors. A patriot can indeed be an immigrant who come in a country and embrace the culture of the country. And learn the history of the country who adopted him and protect and bring more value in the marketplace to rise the country up.

A patriot is an immigrant who respect and loves the country who give him a second chance by respect the rules and regulations establish by our Founding Fathers. A patriot is an immigrant who create jobs and work hard to give back to the country who open the doors for him and his siblings. A patriot is not the one who wanted to destroy his own country and the values of what our Founding Fathers fought to established.

Be a patriot does not mean be only born in the country and did not love the history and culture of the country. A true patriot is the one who absolutely loves is country and who is willing to put on the side hate and false allegations or conspiracy theories about other people. Because they did not look like them do not have the same congregation religion or politics parties. A true patriot is the one who chose to love instead of fear, because fear is the problem and love is the solution. Lun Su ounce said, "when a country fall in chaos patriotism is born". Do you remember Mr. Eugene Goodman? Eugene Goodman is an African American law enforcement officer and U.S Army veteran.

During the insurrection in the United States Capitol Mr. Eugene Goodman was the officer who save the lives of a lot of Senators. This is what we call patriotism. President Kennedy ounce said, "Ask not what your country can do for you, but what you can do for your country. This is what Mr. Eugene Goodman did on January 6, 2021 with this violent mob. He serves his country by putting his life in danger and face the insurrectionists with courage and strategies.

On January 6, 2021, as rioters breached the United States Capitol building, Mr. Eugene Goodman, alone without other officers around him, confronted the rioters himself. He has been cited for heroism in baiting, diversiting and confusing the crowd away from the Senate chamber in the minutes before the chamber could be safely all clear or evacuated. As the crowd reached a landing from which there was an unimpeded path to the Senate chamber, Mr. Goodman pushed the lead rioter and then retreated away from the chamber.

Officer Goodman in few seconds, tricked the violent mob, willingly becoming a trap, pulling them away from the chamber where others armed officers were waiting, by doing that officer Goodman avoiding tragedy and he save the lives of the Lawmakers Republican, Democratic and the Vice-President. Which include his own life and his colleagues lives. This is what we call patriotism and during this event God self-know how many times officer Goodman was cursed and be calling the N word. And he used his reasoning mind and staying calm and focus on his plan to protect all the Lawmakers and his colleagues.

Remember the Capitol was built in 1793 and the lead architect was Thomas Walter, and the free labor was coming from African American slaves. African American Capitol officers are very aware of the racism and injustice it has been going on for years at the government building. Since Woodrow Wilson who brought the segregation in the federal agencies against African American. The insurgency at the Capitol on January 6, 2021 show what we all known. Multiples African American officers have filed racial discrimination suits against the law enforcement agency for years. The African American officers endured a lot of abuse, by white colleagues calling some African American officers the N-word, putting objects in their lockers with racial slurs on it. They refused to be friends with them and one some of them hangout with African American officers they are calling threats. Its was even worse during President Obama terms. One of the white officers audaciously call President Obama monkey, and add go back to Africa. When they bring that to the intention of their leaders they denied, and states is no racism here. Few of the African American officers quit their jobs because of racism in the 21st century.

Chapter 3: Leadership

A leader is the one who lead by example and a leader most have all those qualities:

*Loyal

*Example

*Attitude (positive)

*Determined

*Empathy

*Respect

A leader who does not have those qualities is not a leader, is just a follower. Because the difference between a leader and a follower is that the leader will make some decision the follower cannot make. This great country has been established by amazing leaders and masterminds who took their time to write the U.S Constitution to leave the next generations an outstanding democracy. And what keep happening in this great country is incredibly sad. The Founding Fathers were not perfect, and they did their best to solve some issues do not create them. Therefore, they wrote the Federalist Papers and divided the government with three strongest branches who are basically equal.

After the end of the Civil War on April 9, 1865 one year after in 1866 six ex Generals of the

Confederate Army established in Pulaski

Tennessee the Ku Klux Klan and they elected their

first grand wizard Nathan Bedford Forrest 1867-

1869. Before the war, Forrest amassed a lot of

wealth as a cotton plantation owner, horse and

cattle trader, real estate broker, and slave trader. In

1861 he joined the Confederate Army and became

one of the soldiers during the Civil War to enlist as

a private and be promoted to general without any

prior military training. An expert cavalry leader,

Forrest was given command of a troop and

established new principles for mobile forces,

earning the nickname "The Wizard of the Saddle".

His strategics influenced more generations to come

of military strategists. He got the admiration of the

Confederate high command. Because in April 1864, in what was called "one of the bleakest, saddest events of American military history", troops under Bedford command massacre of over 300 Union troops who had surrendered themselves, almost all were African American soldiers, and few Tennessean fighting for the Union, at the Battle of Fort Pillow. And the Union resolve win the war.

Bedford Forrest joined the KU Klux Klan in 1867 two years after its founding. The Klan group was a loose collection of local factions throughout the former Confederacy that used violence and the threat of violence and intimidation to maintain white supremacists' control over the newly enfranchised former slaves. The Ku Klux Klan,

with Forrest as their leader, suppressed voting

rights of African American in the South with

violence, intimidation and murder during the

presidential elections of 1868.

In 1869, Forrest expressed disillusionment with the

lack of discipline among the nascent white

supremacist terrorist and notorious group

everywhere in the South and Bedford Forrest

decided the eradication of the Ku Klux Klan and

destruction of its white robes (costumes) He then

left the terrorist group he helped to established.

And he lies in public he had never been a member

of the Ku Klux Klan and he aspire in favor of racial

harmony. Did this remind you someone? Could you please stick with me? And you will understand how those bad leaders manipulate their sympathizers and when they got cut lies, they deny their implication.

Chapter 4: Mutation

The mutation is the changing of the structure of a gene, resulting in a variant form that may be transmitted to subsequent generations caused by the alteration of single base units in DNA or the deletion and insertion or rearrangement of large sections of genes or chromosomes. Like those notorious and violent terrorists' groups or organizations in the United States. They just mutate, kept their DNA and venomous, from 1865-2021 they mutate severs times.

 They went from Ku Klux Klan, Jim Crow, White Supremacists, Proud Boys, Qanon or Q , who is a disproven and discredited far-right conspiracy theory alleging that a secret cabal of satan worshipping, cannibalistic pedophiles is running a global child sex trafficking organization and plotted against former United states President Trump while he was in office, Oath Keepers, which claims tens of thousands of present and former law enforcement officials and military veterans as members is one of the largest radical antigovernment groups in the United States today.

The White supremacist groups have killed more people than any other domestic violent extremist group, DHS says. Therefore, all those White supremacist groups when they got exposed. They just acted like snakes start the process of shedding their old skin by rubbing against a rock, tree or similar hard surface. They typically rub a spot by their snout, so they can then slip out their old skin by wriggling against rocks, plants and similar surfaces. Although many White supremacist groups spend a significant amount of time underground(hide) or Southern States and small counties. They usually come up to the surface to shed their skin all White supremacist groups must do this occasionally, typically every 4 years, depending on who is in the office (President) on their growth rate and need more members to adhere.

Chapter 5: Capitol Attack

On January 6, 2021, everything began with the news that the Reverend. Raphael Gamaliel Warnock would make history to become the first African American United States Senator from Georgia, that meant that the Democrats would take control of the Senate with the win also of Jon Ossof who would become the first Jewish Senator of

Georgia. That meant the Democrats would have 50 Senators and the Republicans 50 and the Vice-President Elected Kamala Harris breakdown to give the Democrats the lead in the Senate. Chuck Schumer would become the majority leader and Mitch McConnell would become the minority leader; this pill was harder for the Republicans to swallow. And ended with the country reeling from the aftermath of the insurrection on the Capitol building.

In 2016 after the 45th President was elected, the whole world noticed and witnessed a huge grew of White supremacist and White extremists' groups emerged around the United States. Those violent groups used the same technics as the terrorist groups in middle East and Europe. They used social medias and network channels who are antigovernment, to recruit their members. And must of them are vulnerable mentally with a lack of knowledges. Those members are easy target to corrupted and they are looking for a messiah who share their vision.

Indeed, those recruiters after enrolled the new recruits in their groups. They will brainwash them with absurdities, fear and hate. All this process always take place in videos conferences or they will meet them in their own towns. Then they will train some for come back combat and lie to them, there is a Civil War who is coming you must be prepared to fight for your country. They will often use the emotion of fear to distill their messages knowing those people have only one source of information or network and for some none. By use those methods, those recruiters know repetition is the mother law of learning. Therefore, they will bombard them with false allegations and information's. Until those messages sank in their subconscious minds and accepted.

When their finally adhere those terrorist groups, the new members will try to share the toxic messages with their family's members. And the members who will try to bring them to the truth or reality, will be banned or segregated from the family and their will call him/her enemy. Those new members of those groups will often leave their families members if their do not support their beliefs and established a new family with those notorious groups.

Those recruiters will always remind them to do not worry about any negative or bad action they will take. Because they have the support of all the 3 branches of the government, the Legislative, the Executive and the Judicial. Therefore, every time their attend a manifestation they are so confident. Because inside those 3 branches of the government they have their leaders who give them instructions and sponsor them financially.

Do you remember on August 12, 2017, when James Alex Fields Jr voluntary drove in full speed his car into a crowd of innocent people who had been peacefully protesting in Charlottesville, Virginia killing Heater Heyer and injured more than 19 people? The 20 years old Fields had driven from Ohio to attend the manifestation. Fields previously espoused neo-Nazi and white supremacist beliefs. In July 2019 he was sentenced to life in prison.

Then the leader of a North Carolina based group associated with the Ku Klux Klan says he is happy that Ms. Heater Heyer died while taking part in a rally in Charlottesville, Virginia. And President Trump says, "I think is blame on both sides," the President told reporters that day in August 2017. Only 8 months after his Presidential inauguration as the 45th U.S President. President Trump comments on Charlottesville in 2017 showed his support to the white supremacist. Therefore, this is was one of the reasons why Joe Biden decided to run for the Presidential election in 2020.

On January 6, 2021, what began as a baseless protest the results of the 2020 Presidential election transformed into a violent attack on one of the most powerful buildings in the United States of America. The angry rioters' heaters toward the House who represent the U.S democracy (Capitol) just after President Trump speech at the manifestation he organized near the White House to demonstrate against the certification of President Elect Joe Biden as the 46th President of the United States. On the same time, the lawmakers were voting to certify the electoral votes.

When suddenly President Trump advise his supporters to march to the Capitol and says he will be marching with them as well. After repeating false allegations that the election was rigged and instructing his supporters to "stop the steal." When President Trump supporters was on their way toward the U.S Capitol, law enforcement vehicles went fast to block the mob. At the same time, since 10 am Trump supporters divide themselves in multiple groups, some of them were near the White House, some near the Department of Labor and some at the west and east sides of the Capitol.

They used this strategy to confuse the law enforcement when it is time to strike. They were well organized, they came in Washington, D.C severs times to study the behaviors of the federal law enforcement polices and D.C police (MPD). Also, inside the law enforcement polices and federal agencies, they have their members who give them information.

When the crowd broke through windows, barricades and police checkpoints and ran rampant through the building. I was home watching that on tv, and my son call me, and he asked me if I was aware of what happening in the Capitol. My response was yes, and we cannot believe it. Then my son asks me, "Dad do you think if those people were African American, they will allow them to even reach the steps of the U.S Capitol?" I pause for few seconds to assess the situation and I also knew my son understood the injustice in this marvelous country he was eleven years old. My response was, if its was people who looks like us, we will never even reach the security checkpoints and if we even reach the police checkpoints.

They will send every law enforcement units, National guards and helicopters coming from Virginia, Maryland and D.C include FBI police headquarter who is in less than 2 minutes away from the Capitol. By the way from the west wing of the Capitol you can see the FBI building who was named after John Edgar Hoover who led the FBI between 1924-1972 (48 years). And when this insurrection took place in the Capitol, the director was Christopher Wray.

This is what we call White privileges. One man proudly broke into House Speaker Nancy Pelosi's office and sit down on her chair with his feet up on her desk and stole her email and later will brag that in public with a smile on his face. Another carried

her lectern through the halls, and a young lady stole

her laptop who content important information

regarding the country. The Capitol police used tear

gas into the Rotunda, the Lawmakers were forced

to shelter in place as the minutes becomes hours of

violence.

Lawmakers and their staffs were calling their

families members and make their last wishes. Some

Republicans Lawmakers called on Trump to

instruct his supporters to leave the Capitol building

and to stop the violence. And Trump was watching

everything on tv with his family and some of his

staff members. He later sends a short video on

Twitter, advise them to go home and he love them they are specials. And he repeatedly says, "the election was stolen." After this video Twitter banned Trump permanently from Twitter.

We can hear President Trump mob scanted "hang Mike Pence" his own Vice-President and he never check on him or his family during the insurrection. The Vice-President was few minutes away to face the insurrectionists, thank God to the bravura of some law enforcement who make him, his family members and staff escape this violent mob who was after him. Because he tries the honor the U.S Constitution (the 12 Amendment).

Some of those unbelievable images horrified the world included most of the insurrectionists wearied in t-shirts says, "Make America Great Again or Stop the Steal" we saw them making their way up the 365 steps of the Capitol who represented the 365 days in the years a sacred place. We saw the statue of the freedom facing the east side of the mall. Because the sun rises in the east and go down on the west. Therefore, the sun never goes down under the statue of the freedom.

On January 6, 2021, we saw the smoke cover up the face of the statue of the Freedom, remember where a smoke underneath is fire. And the statue of Peace who is located at the west side of the Capitol, near where the presidential inauguration always takes place every 4 years on January 20. We saw the statue of Peace crying. Because her own sons and daughters was destroying what everybody as in common the democracy. We saw the statue of President Ulysses S. Grant who is located at the west side of the Capitol be disrespected and vandalized maybe by ignorance or lack of knowledge.

Because its was President Grant who save the Union on the field on April 9, 1865 at Appomattox Court House when General Robert E. Lee surrendered his troops to at this time one of the great General of his generation, I say Ulysses S.

Grant who will become the 18 United States President. And you can see his face on the 50-dollar bill. President Ulysses S Grant saw spiritually the Capitol building who represent the U.S democracy be attacked, knowing all his adult life he gives that to his country to fought against injustice, racism and slavery. He fought against the Confederate Army in Chattanooga, Battle of Belmont, Battle of Fort Henry, Battle of Fort, Donelson Battle of Shiloh Vicksburg, Campaign Overland, Campaign Petersburg and Appomattox Campaign; Grant was an exceptional General. Therefore, he will never allow what happened in the Capitol to happen if he was still physically in life.

Because he fought for the democracy of his country to be respected around the world and especially in the United States. He was a great leader who led his Amies by example and not from behind he was on the field. We also saw the statue of President James S. Garfield who is located at the west side of the Capitol be disrespected by the insurrectionists, we saw a police officer's running from mob inside the Capitol building and some even cooperate with the mob. We can hear the noise coming from inside and outside. We saw a confederate flag inside the Capitol building even during the American Civil War 1861-1865 that never happen. The insurrection or attack in the Capitol left at least five Americans dead and thousands of injuries. Three law enforcement officers died, and two insurrectionists lost their lives. The United States who always give advice of democracy to other countries now was under attack by his own citizens and not by a foreign terrorist's groups. Therefore, currently its hard for the U.S to give other countries advice about democracy. Because some American citizens do not believe in his own democracy. The whole world especially the partners of the U.S was willing to come help the Capitol during this attack and by the policy of countries they sign, no countries could do it. Because that will be an interference. Non-interventionism is the diplomatic policy whereby a nation seeks to avoid alliances with other nations in order to avoid being drawn into wars not related to direct territorial self-defense. It has had a long history among elite and popular opinion in the United States. At times, the degree and nature of this policy was better known as isolationism, such as the period between the world wars one and two.

During this insurrection in the United States Capitol over 538 hundred Lawmakers, the staffs, law enforcements and the Vice-Presidents was trap and shelter inside the Capitol for more than 3 hours. The Lawmakers, staffs and law enforcements was traumatized until now they still recovery from this insurrection. When they were shelter in a secure location inside the Capitol can you believe, some Republicans Lawmakers refused to wear their face masks? Knowing we are dealing with a pandemic. The result was few days after couple of Lawmakers and law enforcement officers tested positive to the Covid-19.

The votes resume after Congress reconvened hours after violent insurrectionists storms the Capitol building, forcing party leaders to evacuate the chambers while rioters overtook the Capitol. The Senate Majority Leader Mitch McConnell said as he returned to the Senate floor earlier in the Evening" The United States Senate will not be intimidated, we will not be kept out of this chamber by thugs, mobs or threats. We will not bow to lawlessness or intimidation. We are back at our posts. We will discharge our duty under the Constitution and for our nation and we are going to do it tonight."

The Speaker of the House Nancy Pelosi called the violent insurrectionists an "assault" on democracy and vowed to carry forward with the work of certifying Joe Biden's election win. "We know that we are in difficult times, but little could we have imagined the assault that was on our democracy today. To those who strove deter us from our responsibility, you have failed." Even after they returned to count the electoral votes, some Republicans Lawmakers tried to disturb the

Congress and Senate with those false allegations. They even forget what happening few hours ago because of those lies. This is the memory of the red fish. Then Vice-President Pence announces Joe Biden's victory after Congress completes electoral count.

Therefore, after the insurrection in the Capitol the Pentagon send 20 000 national guards to secure the Capitol. Then few weeks after the Congress impeach Trump for the second time. During this impeachment process, few Republicans vote "Yea" to impeach President Trump. We saw some Lawmakers hiring private security guards because of the reprisals. On January 20, 2021, the

Presidential Inauguration took place at the West wing of the Capitol. The same place where the insurrectionists destroyed during their attack. Every former Presidents attend the inauguration except Jimmy Carter due to his age and President Trump refuse to attend the Presidential inauguration.

He also refuses to concede his lost to the Presidential election. Remember the United Stated Constitution do not mention election concede. For the country's first hundred years or so, conceding a race was not part of the process at all. In politics, a concession is the act of a losing candidate publicly yielding to a winner candidate after the overall result of the vote has been clear. Therefore,

President John Adams a Federalist was the first candidate to concede privately the election to President Thomas Jefferson a Democratic-Republican in 1800. They did not talk for years and died on the same month, day and year on July 4, 1826 within five hours of each other. In 1860, Democrat Stephen Douglas conceded to Republican Abraham Lincoln with those kind words, "Partisan feeling must yield to patriotism. I am with you, Mr. President, and God bless you." The first concession telegram occurred when William Jennings Bryan sent William McKinley two days after the 1896 United States presidential election. Prior to that election results took long time and thus candidates maintained an air of detachment from the process. The telegram was rather brief and read as follow, "Lincoln, Neb., November 5. Hon. Wm. McKinley, Canton, Ohio: Senator jones has just informed me that the returns indicate your election, and I hasten to extend my congratulations. We have submitted the issue to the American people and their will is law." The concession is the celebration of democracy, a reflection on why democracy and the participation of millions of voters in the electoral process is important, and that their choice must be respected.

President Donald Trump has been an exception to the tradition of concession in American presidential politics, refusing to concede defeat and declaring victory for himself despite having lost both the popular vote and electoral college in the 2020 United States presidential election. Biden won 306 electoral votes and the popular votes as well 81 million, Trump won 232 electoral votes and the popular votes 74 million. In the modern years and so recently in 2000, Al Gore a Democrat candidate to the presidential election called the Republican candidate George W. Bush to concede in the early hours after election night only to call back and retract his concession when the race unexpectedly tightened up. Therefore, their first dialogue was compatible and the second was tense, with Al Gore famously telling George W. Bush, "You do not have to get snippy about it."

Chapter 6: Solutions

To solve this issue of false allegations and conspiracy. The three branches of the government: The Legislative, the Executive and the Judicial must be impartial and must stop directly or indirectly to support those violent groups of white supremacists. Because if those groups keep growing in numbers year after years. It is because they are confident that they have the support of all three branches of the government. Therefore, nobody can stop them because they have white privileges.

Therefore, they have the nerf to go at the Capitol and hunt Lawmakers and the Vice-President and sing "Hang Mike Pence". This is unbelievable in a nation like the United States of America, who is the most powerful nation in the world. Those violent and criminal groups they fed for years, now come back after their owners. Because they refuse to acknowledge the situation since the foundation of the Ku Klux Klan, those leaders denied the reality. Imagine if at least 80 or 90% of them accept the reality and act like President Ulysses S. Grant did back in the earlier 1870. A lot of those white supremacist groups will never be existed publicly or will be eradicated from the United States.

During slavery who started at Jamestown currently known as Hampton, Virginia in 1619, after they brought 20 Africans and sold them like animals in the slave's market. Then the Europeans descendants were giving the privilege to own human beings. This is where the white privilege began in one British colony named Virginia and 7 years after New York was founded in 1626. They substitute African names with European names and when Africans refused to comply. They were beating to death or lynched in public to send a message to the next one who refused to cooperate to their Machiavelli technics. Therefore, some Africans developed new technics to keep their identities intact by telling the truth to their kids about their genuine identities and where they are from. Also, they used to give them African names and advise them to fake accepting the names their slave masters give them. Until they were giving the opportunity to fought for their freedoms during the American Civil War April 12, 1861- April 9, 1865. Nobody give them their freedom in a plat they fought for it and millions lost their lives to save the Union and to be free. Because they believe, their grandchildren will live in a country where they did not go to be judge for the color of their skins but for the content of their characters.

The white community especially the one who lead those white supremacist groups, must learn from history and from African American who has been oppressed for 20 score and 2 years until now. Because insanity is doing the same thing over and over and expected a different result ounce says by Albert Einstein, who came in this country in 1932 because he ran the oppression of Adolph Hitler. White or Caucasian leaders must ask themselves this question, did we want to leave the next generations in a country who is divided against himself? President Abraham Lincoln ounce says, "A house who is divided against himself cannot stand."

I do not think white supremacist leaders want to leave to their kids a nation where you are unjustly convicted to a crime or kill because of the color of your skin. I do not think white supremacist leaders want to leave their next generation a country where you are segregate or can not get a federal job because of the skin of your color. This is the time to stop this negative mental attitude because your attitude determines your altitude. And you do not want your kids to pay for what you did. Because you can escape the law of men, but you never escape the Universal Laws because, they were established by Almighty God. You must pay your Karmic debt before you die, and people will remember you by the way you live your life.

Today, someone Presidents or leaders' names nobody wants to be associate with them. Because they did not used their purposes constructively or positively. Life is a journey therefore, you will be judge by God by the way you use your talent, purpose or gift. Remember, like attract like this is the Law of Attraction. Therefore, if you spray lies, you will receive lies in return. You do not attract what you want but you attract who you are ounce says by Dr. Wayne Dyer.

You cannot plant an apple tree and expect to have orange fruits. You will always ripe double of what you sow this is the Law of Abundance. Your words are powerful, you must use them wisely and before you speak assess the situation. Because your words

can incite people who belief in you to act.

Therefore because of the words of one man the

whole world went in a war who kill over 70 to 85

million people between 1939-1945. Today few

people want to be associate to Hitler name even his

own children or partners. He destroys himself his

legacy.

Only God knows how many leaders close their

eyes and hears when African Americans face

challenging times since 1619 thru 2021. They were

thinking this is not their problems, and behind close

doors they activate or motivate white supremacist

groups to continue their atrocities against a

community who just ask to respect what is write in paper, the 14 Amendment Equal Protection of The Laws. Because they manipulate the people for so long now the beast, they feed for so long do not have nothing to eat. Because African Americans develop new methods to avoid being eat, now the beast he is coming to attack his owners. You will never look good by making someone else look bad, the energy you put out there will come back to you.

Remember life is energy, therefore 90% of our bodies content water and everything vibrate in different frequencies. By example if you want to listen a specific radio station like 9.1 you must tune to the right frequency 9.1 if you want to listen the content of this radio. Therefore, the same process happens with human beings. Remember the towel who dry your buttock today, will be the same towel who will dry your face tomorrow. Therefore, you must be careful of incited people to do negative stuffs. Because those same people will come bac after you one day. Remember who kill by the sword will be kill by the same sword. And when you spit on the sky the same spit will come back at your face or body. A country is on the image of his leader. The pathology who made this country sick is in himself is not a foreign country. When the leaders of this great country will change the way, they look at their citizens, their citizens will change.

Remember you cannot change nobody, but you can change your thoughts, habits and attitudes. Therefore, after they change themselves first, by putting love in the center of everything fear will vanish, and the emotion of love will take place. Because your mind can not be occupied on the same time by two emotions one will always dominate. Therefore, they must call a wrong action wrong and not try to polish by calling right and caress the authors of those actions. Because if you keep doing that, the same actions will always produce the same results. Therefore, you will keep running at the same place," Rat race." Because life will teach you the same lesson over and over until you get it right.

Most of those people who attacked the Capitol on January 6, 2021 are still home waiting for their process. Over 270 people was identified and only few has been arrested. Imagine if those citizens were African Americans, all of them will be arrested and put in jail. This is the reality of this beautiful country the justice is not equal, and we have the 14 Amendment. For the same crime, an African American will be condemned for 7 years in prison and a Caucasian only 2 years for the same crime different sentences. This is white privileges and now do you understand the double standard in this country?

This is one of the reasons why Frederick Douglass, Harriet Tubman, Booker T. Washington, W.E.B Du Bois, Charles W. Chesnutt, Dunbar, Marcus Mosiah. Garvey, Ruby Bridges, Dr. Martin Luther. King Jr, Malcolm X, Sam Cooke, Al Sharpton, Thurgood Marshall, John Lewis, Elijah Cummings, Barack Obama, Raphael Warnock, Stacey Abraham and Kamala Harris fought for equal justice and civil rights. To cure this pathology, we must dive deeper thru is source and then provide the appropriated medications to eradicate this pathology who disgrace the image of the country around the world. Because if you skip this gold chance or opportunity to solve this issue now. You will be running all your life when another issue will appear and try to blame other people instead of facing.

The Universe give so many occasions to the leaders of this country to solve this issue of white supremacists. And the three branches of the government keep walking away until that happen to them in broad day light. Even now we still have some people including some Lawmakers who witness the attack themselves in the Capitol. And they still denied the reality and try to blame other people, when everybody knows who attack the capitol this is insane. Therefore, you should never try to convince a pessimist person. Because for the pessimist the glass is half empty and for the optimist the glass is half full. Therefore, both are right because they are victim of their own beliefs. The pessimist is hostage of his ego and the optimist a host to God. In Africa we have a proverb who says, "Washing the hands of a monkey with the soap is wasting the soap." Because the monkey will always go dirty his hands, and I desire people do not take this proverb in the first degree.

In conclusion, when our Founding Fathers founded this marvelous nation was with the desire that all men are create equal. Also, all men can have the same rights and opportunities to succeed and to protect this nation. Therefore, always remember that love is the solution of every problem we create ourselves with our beliefs and fear is an illusion that is created by ourselves coming from our own beliefs. Therefore, fear is the problem. We must leave a nation where is love for the next generations because our kids will value what we value.